WHY DON'T I HAVE A DADDY?
A Story of Donor Conception

GEORGE ANNE CLAY
Illustrated by Lisa Krebs

AuthorHouse™
1663 Liberty Drive, Suite 200
Bloomington, IN 47403
www.authorhouse.com
Phone: 1-800-839-8640

First published by AuthorHouse 7/14/2008

ISBN: 978-1-4259-9587-4 (sc)

Library of Congress Control Number: 2007902283

Printed in the United States of America
Bloomington, Indiana

This book is printed on acid-free paper.

authorHOUSE®

To George

My little lion cub – who is more wonderful
than I ever imagined he would be.

Acknowledgements

The main impetus for this book was my desire to help my son understand his origins. However, it also quickly became a testament of how much he is loved by so many. With family members and friends lending their support and advice, the book also carries a message of love. While many helped in the process, I want to acknowledge a few of the most pivotal individuals.

My sister, Jeanne Dickerson, transformed the concept of writing a children's book about donor conception from just a nice idea to a do-able reality. Her input into the writing and her editing comments were instrumental as well. With her background in counseling families, she pushed for a very straightforward treatment of the subject, understanding a child's need for truth. I feel I should share the title of author with her for all she has added to this book.

The beautiful artwork in this book is the work of my niece, Lisa Krebs, who spent countless hours bringing the text to life with her illustrations. Her work beautifully illuminates the story and, for a child, the pictures say more than the words. Having his cousin paint the pictures for the book has endeared the book even more to my son.

My mother encouraged us every step of the way, believing that this book should be available to other single mothers as they educate their own children about their origins. It was through her support that this book was published.

I also must thank other family members and friends for their insights and encouragement at various stages. All of my family and friends have been so loving and supportive, not just of this book but, more importantly, of my son and me. They have enveloped us with their love and encouraged pride in our family of two.

And finally, I must thank a man, whose name I do not know, for his generosity. It is thanks to his gift that I have a wonderful son.

"Where are you? I know you are hiding …" the mama lion called out to her cub as they played in the tall grass. Just then the little lion pounced from behind a rock and roared as loud as he could.

"Did I surprise you, Mama?" the cub asked gleefully.

"Oh my, yes you did!" the mama lion said as she laughed.

The little lion ran to find a new hiding place, but stopped to watch some zebras gallop across the plain. "Mama," he called to his mother, "there are a lot of zebras in that family. One, two, three, four, five, six, seven!"

"Good job counting. There are seven in that family - a mommy, a daddy and five little ones," the mama lion replied.

The mama lion and her cub continued on until they came to the water's edge for a nice cool drink. On the other bank was a large herd of elephants, squirting water at each other. "Here is another family," the mama lion said as she watched the elephants play.

"It looks like there is a mommy, a daddy, a grandmother, a grandfather and five grandchildren in this elephant family. The grandmother elephant seems to be just as proud watching the young elephants splash about as your grandmother is when she watches you practice roaring." In response, the little cub practiced his roar and trotted off, with his mama close behind.

Further on they wandered past a beautiful panther playing with a little leopard who was climbing on her back. "Mama," the little lion cub remarked, "they don't look like they belong together."

"Well, honey, the little leopard didn't have a mommy or daddy leopard that could care for her. Instead the panther has become the little leopard's mommy. She is the one who takes care of the little leopard. Animals do not have to look like each other in order to be in the same family. It is the love they share that makes them a family. You can tell the panther and leopard love each other. Look at how they laugh and smile. The little leopard laughs like her mommy, even though she does not look like her mommy."

"But Mama, will I look like
you when I grow up?"

"In some ways you will be the same…
you have eyes like mine and your
coat is the same golden color…but
you will be different too. Partly you
are different because you are a male
cub, and when you are a grown-up
lion, you'll have a fine, full mane."

Just then a monkey howled overhead in
the tree above the lions. A baby clung to
the mother's back as she swung across
the branches to meet the daddy monkey.

The little lion laughed in
surprise, "Mommy, there are
families all over the place!"

"Yes," the mama replied. "Yet, no two
families are exactly the same, just as no
two animals are exactly the same."

The lion cub thought about all the different families he had seen, and thought about his own family. His family had two lions, his mother and him, but no daddy. Wondering about this, the little cub asked, "Mama, why don't I have a daddy?"

"Well, yours is a special story. I had you on my own because I did not have a daddy for you. For you see, my little one, you have always been in my heart. I wanted and loved you soooo much, even before I knew how truly wonderful you would be," the mama lion said as she lovingly licked the cub's soft fur.

"But that is not your whole story," the mama lion continued. "Each animal is created by a female and a male, a mother and a father. Kind of like when you mix yellow and blue, you get the color green, a new and separate color. Even though I chose to have you and care for you on my own, I needed the help of a male lion to create you. The male lion who helped create you is your father. So while you have no "daddy" that lives with you, there is a lion who is your father. He is not part of our lives, but in some ways he is part of you. Just like the color blue is part of the color green."

"I have a father?" the little lion asked with surprise, because he had only known his mother's love, her strong face, her warm embraces. There was no daddy that cared for him and played with him.

"Yes, you have a father who helped create you. But, not all cubs know the parents that created them," the mama lion explained. "You know me, your mother, your mommy, but you do not know your father. You do not know him because he is a donor. A donor is a lion who helps another lion by giving a gift. The donor lion gave a doctor some of his sperm, which is his special seed for making babies. The doctor then gave this special seed to me. Eventually, I gave birth to you, a strong baby lion."

"But who is my father?" asked the little cub eager to learn all that he could.

"I have never met your father and do not even know his name." the mama lion answered. "You see, one of the rules for receiving this special gift from a donor lion is that both the mother and the cub are not able to meet the donor father. Also, your donor father does not even know about us. However, I do have some information about him. I know he is strong and likes to run fast. I also know he must be a kind and generous lion because he helped make your life possible. So, my dear sweet cub, you were created out of my strong, deep love for you and the generous gift of a special lion."

This was a lot for the little cub to think about. He always told other lion cubs that he didn't have a daddy, but now he knew he had a father. "Mama, what am I supposed to say when other cubs ask about my daddy?"

"Well, let's see. What I tell adult lions is that I had you on my own with the help of a donor. I think you could simply say, 'we don't have a daddy in our family. My family is my mom and me.' It may be hard for some cubs to understand that you don't have a daddy when they have dads who are important to them.

As you get older you might want to explain to your friends that there is someone who is your father, but you do not know him because he is a donor. He does not know you either and is not able to be a part of your life." The mama lion gave her cub a big tight squeeze and said, "I am the lucky one who can hug you each and every day."

"What matters most is how much love you share with others, not the number of animals in your family. We may be a small family compared to the zebras and elephants, but we share so much love between the two of us.

Also, you and I are part of even a larger family. This larger family includes your grandparents, aunts, uncles, cousins, and many dear friends who love us very much." The mama lion spoke as she brushed some grass away from the cub's face. "we are truly blessed."

Looking out at all the different animals roaming over the great plain, the mama lion continued, "Yes, each animal has its own story of how it came to be and who is a part of its family. You came into this world with the help of a donor lion. I will always be thankful for him because he made it possible for me to have you. And I will always be thankful that I had you the way I did. If it had been any different, you would have been a different lion cub, and I love you just the way you are."

The little cub rested his head on his mother's paw,
looked up and purred, "Mama, I love you. I love our family."

A Note to the Grown-Ups...

This book was written out of love. It was created from the love a mother has for her son and the love a family has for the two of them. This love ripples out, touching the lives of many, including you and your child. Seeing yourself as part of this larger family and supported by love is key to having a strong foundation. Make use of this love as you encounter the challenges of parenting a child who does not know his or her father.

There are many challenges with bringing up a child in a world that does not fully understand and support donor conception. Many of them can leave a child or family feeling like something is wrong because they are different. Some parents react by feeling ashamed and keep quiet. Other parents feel the loss and try to make up for it. Both of these strategies can be harmful to you and your child. Instead look for the ways your family is similar to others. Like other families you share love, go to school, work, etc. Even more importantly, recognize that other families have losses too. Not having a father that lives with you is your own unique version of loss. Learning to cope with this loss can be healthy for children. In fact, it gives children an opportunity to learn skills that can serve them a lifetime. As a result they become stronger, more mature and more compassionate than some of their peers who have not had to cope with personal losses.

The strong desire to want to protect your child from hurt can also impact what you choose to tell your child about how he or she was conceived. The tendency is to delay or avoid telling the truth thinking that it will be less harmful. Examples of this are children who are led to believe that their fathers are dead or their step-fathers are their biological fathers. In other cases children are given little or no information at all. Often behind these parenting strategies is the belief that children need to be older to cope with this difficult truth in their lives. Unfortunately, this approach backfires. It is never easy to deal with a hard truth no matter how old a person is. In fact, the older a person is, the greater the shock value, leaving a child feeling like he or she was living a lie. Trust also becomes an issue as a child realizes that the people he or she loves most were perpetuating this lie.

The safest approach is to follow your child's lead, responding to the questions he or she asks. This is your opportunity to speak the truth using words your child can comprehend at his or her level. This book can be a tool to help children work through some of the complexities of their situation. Do not worry if they appear disinterested. As their understanding increases, they will often come back to this book, initiating conversations and expressing an interest in the topic. Having this book available can be one way you have of saying you are open to having this discussion and helping your child process this truth.

Keep in mind that your perspective may be different from your child's. Your perspective may be "there is no father." After all, you brought this child into the world by yourself. Your child's perspective may be different. Most children have difficulty feeling that they are "fatherless," and logically know as they get older that this is not even possible. Be sensitive to these differences and attend to the emotions that go along with them. You may find it easier to speak to these differences using the language in the book. "Father" can be used to speak about a biological father and "daddy" can be used to talk about a father who provides care. This way a child has a father even though that child may not have a daddy who lives with him or her.

As a mother you do not have to make up for not having that "daddy" in your household. Be the loving and courageous mother you are. There can be no doubt of the depth of your love, taking the steps you did to bring your child into this world. Your child knows this and will always be grateful to you. Continue to be courageous in speaking and living the truth. Do not worry about the differences between your family and those around you. Value these differences as the very thing that makes your family special. There is a strong bond that you share with your child because of the decisions you made. Nurture this bond. You are a mom; you gave your child life, and the two of you have a strong and loving relationship. This was not a selfish act but a life-giving act. You can help your child grow from this experience, fostering a more compassionate, sensitive, and loving child. As a result the world is a better place. Love grows, expands, and touches the lives of many.

May your journey together be filled with love, growth, and tender moments.

Jeanne

Jeanne A. Dickerson MA, LCPC, CPCC
Licensed Clinical Professional Counselor
Certified Professional Co-Active Coach

Made in United States
North Haven, CT
24 October 2021